ABC SCHOOL Riddles

Compiled and edited by **Susan Joyce**

Illustrated by **Freddie Levin**

An ABC Riddles book from **Peel Productions**

Published by Peel Productions, Inc.
PO Box 546, Columbus NC 28722
http://peelbooks.com

Printed in Hong Kong

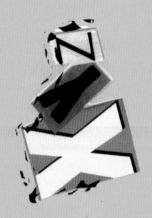
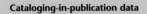

Cataloging-in-publication data

ABC school riddles / compiled and edited by Susan Joyce.
  Illustrations by Freddie Levin
  p. cm.
  "An ABC riddles book."
  ISBN 0-939217-54-6 (alk. paper)
    1. Riddles, Juvenile. [1. Riddles.] I. Joyce, Susan, 1945-

PN6371.5 .A27 2000
398.6--dc21   00-055771

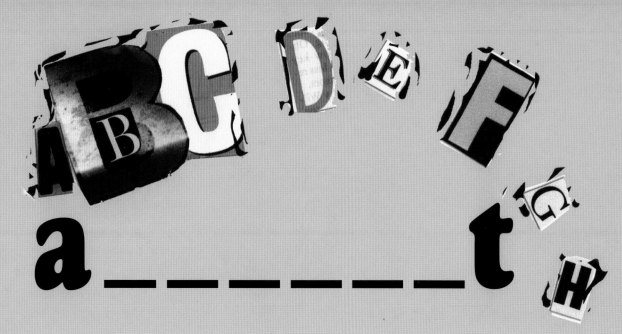

a_____t

I start with an A and end with a T.
To know how to read, you have to know me.
You can spell the word jet
using letters from my set.
There are twenty-six of me.
What can I be?

Robert David Jacobs Jr. • *Richmond, VA*

b___n

I start with a B
and end with an N.
I'm something you use,
again and again.
I help you learn stuff—
both simple and tough.
Find me in your head.
I'm not made of lead.
You store things in me.
What can I be?

Sara Bentley • Springfield, TN

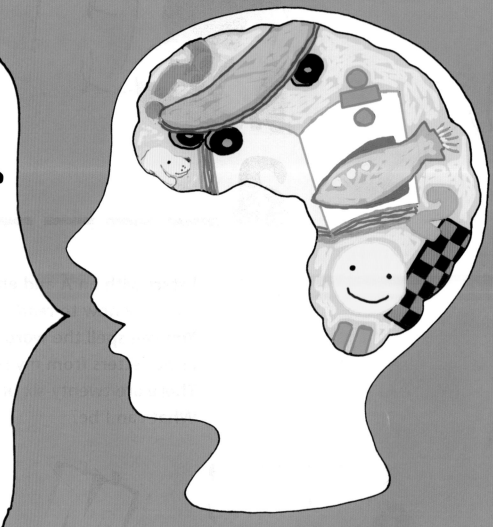

I begin with a C and end with an R.
In case you're wondering, I'm not a car.
I never eat or drink,
but I can read and think.
I save letters and much more—
math games and your score.
You can own me for a fee.
What am I? Can you name me?

c_____r

Adam C. Whitehouse • Tryon, NC

d _ _ _

This hard, handy thing begins with a D.
Sometimes it feels like a prison to me.
But into it, I quickly fit
when the teacher says, "Please sit!"
It is where I stay and write
about why I shouldn't fight.
When my school work is done,
I can draw and have fun.
This is where I'll mostly be.
Can you name me?

Katherine Sellers • Ochlocknee, GA

A | B-C | D-E | F-G | H-J | K-L | M

I start with an E and end with an A.
Find me on a shelf where I sit on display.
I'm something you use
for any subject you choose.
Get information for free
about a frog or a tree.
Most teachers have a set of me.
What can I be?

e_____a

Mary Orczykowski • Washington, MI

I start with an F
and end with a D.
For better or worse,
you always like me.
You like to play basketball,
just like me.
You've got a good dribble,
just like me.
We play ball together,
no matter the weather.
You can always count on me.
What can I be?

f_ _ _ _ _ d

Malcolm Hannon • Tryon, NC

I'm five letters long and start with a G.
Find letters and symbols all over me.
In the shape of a sphere,
I show countries, far and near.
On a table or the ground,
you can spin me round and round.
I show the earth, but not the sky.
Can you guess? What am I?

g _ _ _ _

Sam Bayham • Louisville, OH

h_____k

It begins with an H and ends with a K.
If you want to play, better do it right away.
If you dare forget it,
you'll live to regret it.
Make sure you've done it right,
before going to bed at night,
or you'll be real sorry.
What can it be?

Matthew Losego • Midlothian, VA

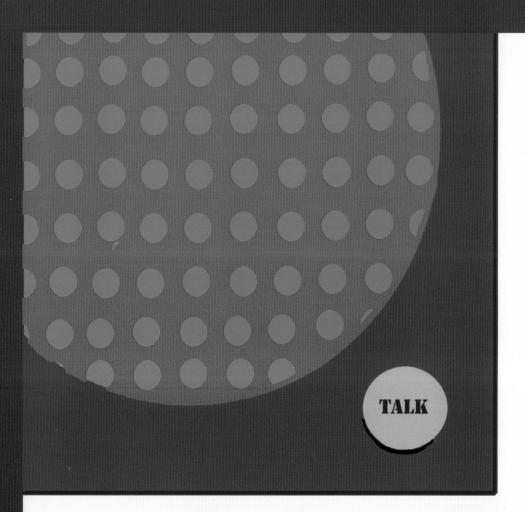

I start with an I
and end with an M.
Hear me everywhere—
in the hall, in the gym.
My sound is abrupt,
when I interrupt.
Find me on the wall.
I'm always on call.
I magnify your voice.
Can you guess?
What's your choice?

i_____m

Richard Anthony Peña • Elizabeth, NJ

j_____l

I start with a J and end with an L.

When you write in me, you learn how to spell.

You can draw and doodle too,

anything you want to do.

Put ideas in me,

only your eyes will see.

What, oh what, can I be?

Carlos Z. Martinoz • Villa Park, IL

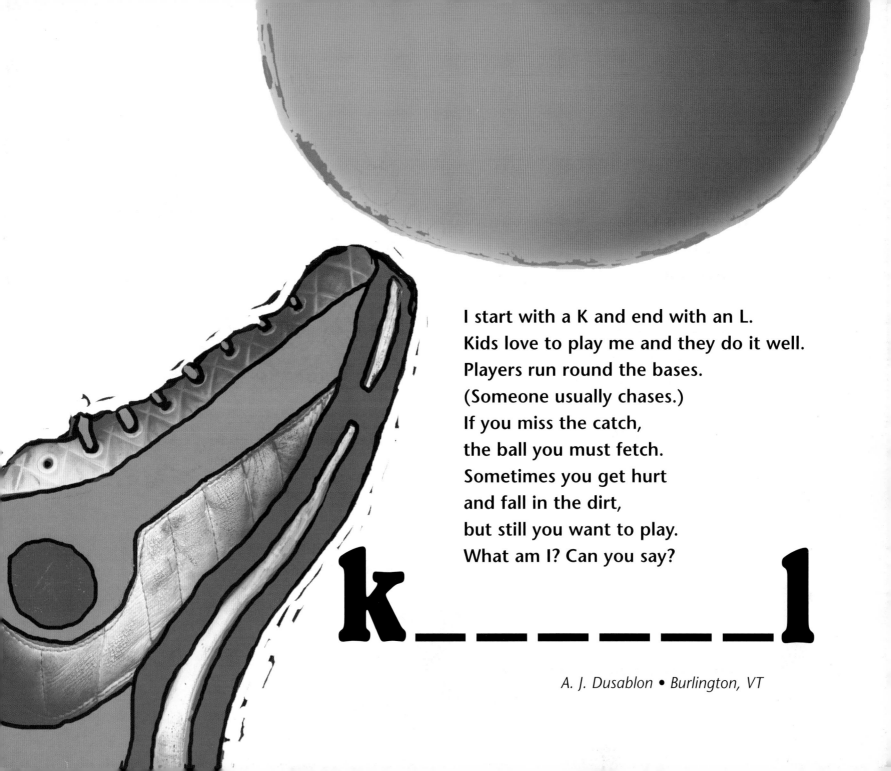

I start with a K and end with an L.
Kids love to play me and they do it well.
Players run round the bases.
(Someone usually chases.)
If you miss the catch,
the ball you must fetch.
Sometimes you get hurt
and fall in the dirt,
but still you want to play.
What am I? Can you say?

k _ _ _ _ _ _ l

A. J. Dusablon • Burlington, VT

I start with an L
and end with a Y.
I'm a place filled
with knowledge—
don't pass me by.
I hold treasures galore—
art, adventure, and more.
When you open your mind,
many things you will find.
Learn of places faraway.
What am I? Can you say?

l_____y

C. Brian Benson II • Whitehouse, TN

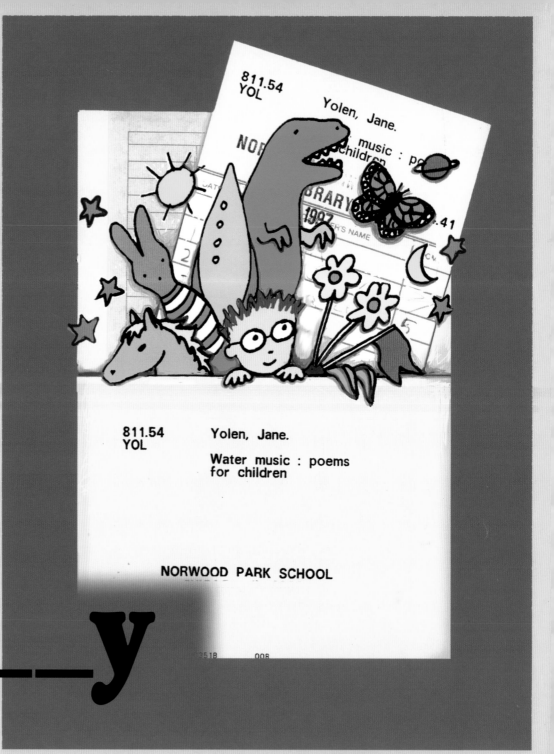

I'm eleven letters long and start with an M.
You need to know me to sing a new hymn.
You need to know me to read a clock,
to figure your height, or measure a dock.
I'm something you learn in every grade.
You better know me, if you want to get paid.
Addition, subtraction, multiplication, division...
Give it a guess. What's your decision?

Kariann K. Beebe • Southbury, CT

m_____

n____e

I start with an N and end with an E.
If you are healthy, you'll never need me.
But if you must rest
(not to escape a test),
or if you are ill,
or if you need a pill,
or have a hurt knee,
stop by and see me.
I'll fix you up—from head to toe.
Who am I? Do you know?

Ashley Ortega • Plainfield, IL

o_ _ _ _ e

I start with an O and end with an E.
All sorts of people work inside me.
Secretaries, treasurers, principals, too—
they're busy working the whole day through.
A school can't run without one of me.
Can you guess? What can I be?

Peter Steusloff • San Diego, CA

p_ _ _ _l

I start with a P and end with an L.
I'm useful when you have a story to tell.
Sometimes I'm yellow; sometimes I'm red;
sometimes you use me to scratch your head.
I'm a very special tool—
used at home and at school.
Don't be a lead head like me.
Get my point?   What can I be?

Alexandra Aird • Kingston, NY

q_ _ _

I'm four letters long and start with a Q.
I'm something short that you must do.
Studying is the main key,
without it you could get a D.
But if you pass me with an A,
I could really make your day.
I often come unexpectedly.
What am I? Can you name me?

Erica L. Briggs • Shickshinny, PA

I start with an R
and end with an S.
I'm something you do
to get rid of stress.
A fun time of day,
when you run and play,
when you dance about,
or play tag and shout.
When the whistle blows, I'm through.
It's back to school work for you.
Solve the riddle. Ready, set, go!
Make your guess. Do you know?

r_____s

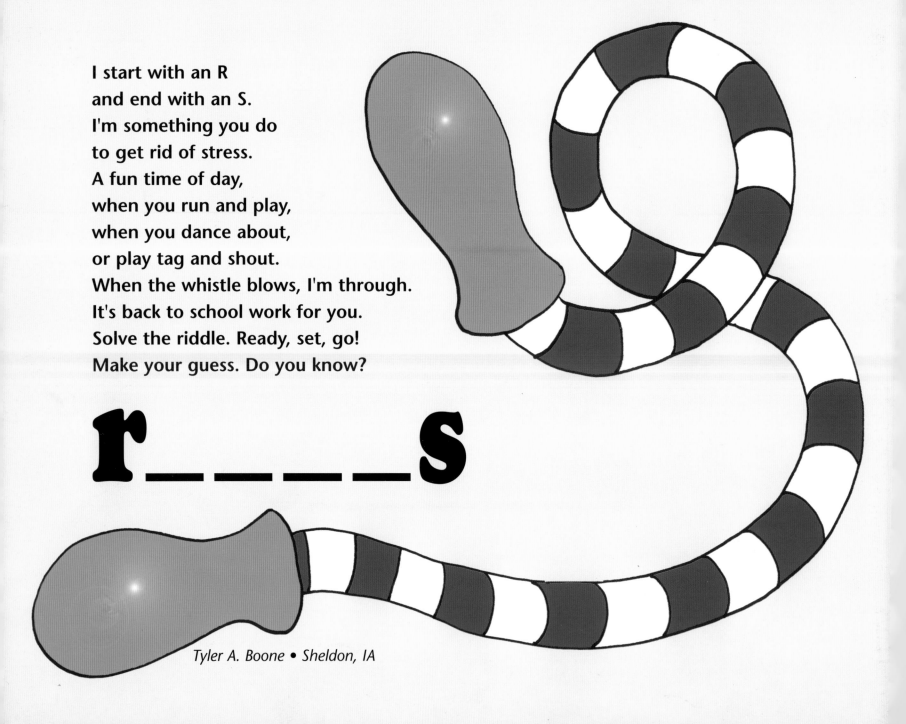

Tyler A. Boone • Sheldon, IA

I start with an S and end with a T.
A teacher has far too many of me.
I need eight hours of rest,
if I want to do my best.
Too much homework drives me crazy.
I would like to just be lazy.
But study hard is what I do.
What am I? Can you guess who?

s_____t

Rachel M. Clark
Cottontown, TN

t_____

I'm seven letters long and start with a T.
I can be short and fat, or tall and skinny.
My number one goal
is to enrich your soul.
On school days, I help you
learn to read and write, too.
What am I? Can you guess who?

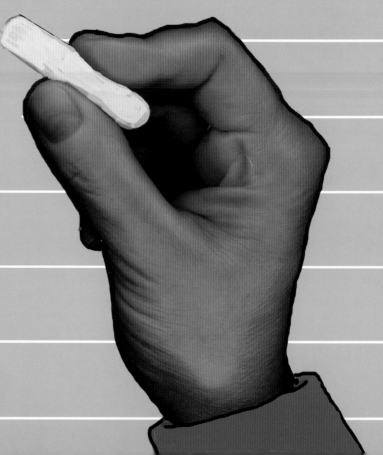

Alan Kramer • Fredericksburg, TX

I start with a U and end with an M.
If I am new, I might need a hem.
Plaid, striped, or plain blue,
I'll look good on you.
Better wear me to school,
if it's the school rule,
or to a ball game
to all look the same.
Most parents like me. What can I be?

u_____m

Gittel Tova Weiss • Staten Island, NY

v_____y

I start with a V and end with a Y.

The more you know of me, the higher you'll fly.

I'm the words that you use

in any subject you choose.

Study me for a quiz.

and you'll be a word whiz.

You'll do great on your test

and score above the rest.

Your grades will be high.

Can you guess? What am I?

Kristi McShane • Villa Park, IL

W_ _ _ _ W

I start with a W and end with one, too.
I'm put in the wall, for kids to look through.
Don't stare out my glass,
instead of listening in class.
You might get in trouble
and your teacher might double
the work you must do.
Can you guess who?

Elizabeth Scheiding • Florissant, MO

X_____e

I start with an X and end with an E.
Children just love to keep hitting me.
In the music room I rest,
always ready to sound my best.
You can play a song on me.
What can I be?

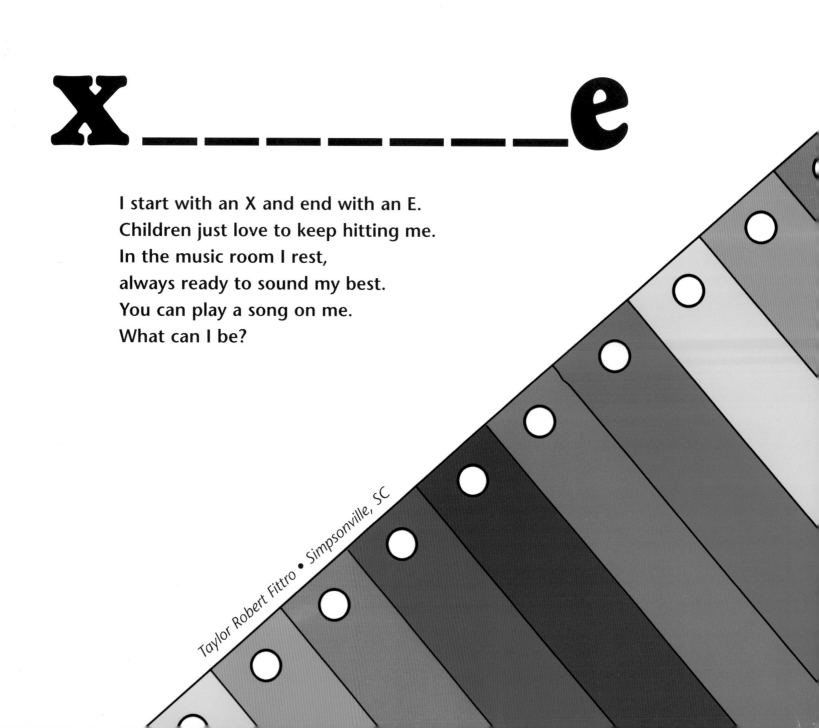

Taylor Robert Fittro • Simpsonville, SC

y————————

Remember Chemistry class? Me Tarzan HA HA!

2 good 2 B 4 gotten

I'm eight letters long, and I start with a Y.
I save memories of the year that's gone by.
I remind you of past trends
with photos of your friends.
Kids write messages in me.
What can I be?

You're the latest—Let's be friends, OK?

I hate to say goodbye... so ... best to you, there

We have fun this summer at the pool and ever...

Don't ever change—great the kid you are!

Kate Wiebke
Marion, IA

Z___O

I start with a Z and end with an O.
Get me on a test, and I'm your worst foe.
My meaning is none.
Hope you don't get one!
I'm nothing you see.
What can I be?

Michael Fader • Levitton, NY

Adam C. Whitehouse

Gittel Tova Weiss

Alan Kramer

Kariann K. Beebe

Malcolm Hannon

Katherine Sellers

Taylor Robert Fittro

Elizabeth Scheiding

Erica L. Briggs

Matthew Losego

Photos not available:

Sara Bentley
Richard Anthony Peña
C. Brian Benson II
Ashley Ortega
Kristi McShane
Michael Fader
Rachel M. Clark

Sam Bayham

Alexandra Aird

A. J. Dusablon

Kate Wiebke

Peter Steusloff

Tyler A. Boone

Mary Orczykowski

Bobby Jacobs

Carlos Z. Martinoz

Sarah Waniak

alphabet	journal	student
brain	kickball	teacher
computer	library	uniform
desk	mathematics	vocabulary
encyclopedia	nurse	window
friend	office	xylophone
globe	pencil	yearbook
homework	quiz	zero
intercom	recess	

Ideas for Parents and Teachers

As a young child, I had dyslexia and had a difficult time reading, writing, and speaking words. Fortunately, my parents believed that children could learn language lessons and be entertained at the same time. So, as a family, we played a word game we called Alphabet Riddles. We would make up rhyming-word riddles whenever we had a few minutes to spare. It made learning words and creating rhyming riddles fun!

In writing workshops across the United States, I have introduced children to the alphabet riddle format. Like magic, it works! Kids love playing with words and making up their own rhyming riddles.

Peel Productions invited students to participate in a nationwide contest to create riddles on the subject of school. 1,368 entries were received from 32 states. 27 winners were chosen representing 17 different states.

As parents and teachers, you can join the fun of making up riddles, too.

- Encourage children to create their own school riddles. Let them choose subjects they like. Begin with letter and word clues. Start with a simple riddle such as:

  I start with a B and end with a D.
  Teachers are always writing on me.

- Stretch the exercise. Look up definitions in the dictionary. Find pictures of the subjects or objects. Add more lines with more clues to the riddle. End each riddle with a question, inviting others to answer the riddle.

- Share riddles! Most written riddles can be solved independently, but it's always more fun to try them out on other people. So, write down the riddles and see if others can figure them out.

- Instruct children to wait until all clues have been given before guessing the riddle. Have the child who guesses the answer first say the correct word, spell it out, and then make up a new school riddle.

- As an extended activity, encourage children to draw the subjects of their riddles.

Have fun with school riddles!

Susan Joyce

s_ _ _ _l

I start with an S; I end with an L.
I begin and end with the ring of a bell.
While here you will learn
to wait for your turn.
You'll learn right from wrong,
and how to get along.
You'll learn to read and spell.
What am I? Can you tell?

Sarah Waniak • Kendal Park, NJ

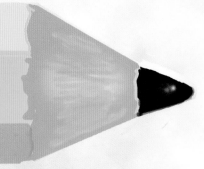

If you've enjoyed this book, look for others, including Alphabet Riddles, on our web site

www.peelbooks.com

or at your favorite bookseller.